C000148245

Turner & Co Productions and paper/scissors/stone in association with Upstart present

MICROCOSM

by MATT HARTLEY

First performed at Soho Theatre, London, on 7 May 2014

CAST

Christopher Brandon	Police Officer
John Lightbody	Philip
Philip McGinley	Alex
Jenny Rainsford	Clare

CREATIVE TEAM

Derek Bond	Director
James Perkins	Designer
Sally Ferguson	Lighting Designer
Jo Walker	Sound Designer
William Newman for IOGIG	Production Manager
George Hims	Stage Manager
Peter Huntley for 1505	Casting

THANKS

We are immensely grateful to everyone who has supported this production. We would like to thank everyone at Soho Theatre, Arts Council England, Hilary Williams, Sally Scott, the Really Useful Group, Tom Stoppard, Angela Hyde-Courtney, Peter Huntley, Jeremy Woodhouse, Tara Finney, Vicky Graham and everyone who supported us via WeFund.

CAST

CHRISTOPHER BRANDON POLICE OFFICER
Christopher trained at LAMDA. Theatre credits include: *Moon Tiger* (Theatre Royal Bath); *The Great Gatsby* (Wilton's Music Hall); *Three Men in a Boat* (Original Theatre); *Mixed Marriage* (Finborough); *The Charming Man, Mad Funny Just* (Theatre503); *50 Ways to Leave Your Lover* (Bush); *Curse of the Starving Class* (Lyceum); *A Midsummer Night's Dream, Timon of Athens* (Shakespeare's Globe); *Henry V* (Manchester Royal Exchange); *As You Like It* (Sheffield Crucible) and *When Five Years Pass* (Arcola). Television credits include: *Endeavour* and *MI High*.

JOHN LIGHTBODY PHILIP
Theatre credits include: *A Midsummer Night's Dream* (Lyric Hammersmith/Manchester Royal Exchange); *Sixty-Six Books* (Bush); *Ghost Stories* (Duke of York's); *Three Sisters* (Lyric Hammersmith/Filter); *Treasure Island* (Theatre Royal Haymarket); *The English Game* (Headlong); *Richard III* (Southwark); *Jane Eyre* (Shared Experience); *Twelfth Night, A Doll's House, Huddersfield* (West Yorkshire Playhouse); *The Taming of the Shrew, Measure for Measure, Richard III* (RSC); *Beautiful People* (Stephen Joseph); *A Christmas Carol, The Sea* (Chichester Festival Theatre); *As You Like It* (National Theatre); *The Admirable Crichton* (Sheffield Crucible/Chichester) *Mansfield Park* (Chichester/tour); *As You Like It, Incarcerater* (BAC); *Romeo and Juliet* (Stray Theatre) and *She Stoops to Conquer* (Northern Stage). Television credits include*: The Musketeers, DCI Banks, Holby City, Doctors Dalziel and Pascoe, Midsomer Murders, The Royal* and *The Bill*. Film credits include: *A Bunch of Amateurs, How to Lose Friends and Alienate People, The Lady of Sorrows, Domestics, The Stick Up* and *Maybe Baby*.

PHILIP MCGINLEY ALEX

Theatre credits include: *The Daughter in Law*, *Hobson's Choice* (Sheffield Crucible); *Straight* (Sheffield/Bush); *Herding Cats* (Hampstead/Ustinov, Bath); *Canary* (ETT/Liverpool Playhouse/Hampstead); *More Light* (Arcola); *The Changeling* (Cheek by Jowl); *Great Expectations* (RSC) and *Kes* (Manchester Royal Exchange). Television credits include: *Drifters*, *Game of Thrones*, *The Gemma Factor*, *Coronation Street*, *Cold Blood*, *Blue Murder*, *Heartbeat*, *Casualty*, *The Bill*, *Falling*, *The Deputy* and *Dalziel and Pascoe*. Film credits include: *Almost Married*; *Prometheus*; *Molehills and How to Get Mugged*.

JENNY RAINSFORD CLARE

Jenny trained at RADA. Theatre credits include *The Little Black Book* (Park Theatre); *The Seagull* (Headlong); *No Quarter* (Royal Court); *Straight* (Sheffield/Bush) and *The Importance of Being Earnest* (Rose Theatre, Kingston). Television credits include *The Smoke* and *Da Vinci's Demons*. Film credits include *About Time*, *Death of a Farmer* and *Prometheus*.

CREATIVE TEAM

MATT HARTLEY WRITER
Matt grew up in the Peak District and studied drama at the
University of Hull. His first play *Sixty Five Miles* won a
Bruntwood Award in the inaugural Bruntwood Competition
and was produced by Paines Plough/Hull Truck. Other work
for theatre includes: *Horizon* (National Theatre Connections);
The Bee (Edinburgh Festival); *Punch* (Hampstead/Heat and
Light Company); *Epic, Trolls, Life for Beginners* (Theatre503).
Radio credits include: *The Pursuit* (Radio 4). Television credits
include: *Hollyoaks*. Matt is currently under commission to the
Royal Shakespeare Company and is a recipient of a T.S. Eliot
commission from the Old Vic Theatre.

DEREK BOND DIRECTOR
Recent theatre credits include: *Shiver* by Daniel Kanaber and
Lost in Yonkers by Neil Simon (Watford Palace Theatre); *Floyd
Collins* by Adam Guettel and Tina Landau (Southwark
Playhouse; winner: Best Musical Production, Off West End
Awards; nominated: Best Musical, Evening Standard Theatre
Awards). Derek was associate director at Theatre503 from
2010–2011 where credits included: *Many Moons* by Alice Birch
and *PLAYlist* (Theatre503/Latitude Festival/Live Theatre
Newcastle). Other credits include: *Saraband* by Ingmar
Bergman (Jermyn Street); *Trying* by Joanna McLelland Glass
(Finborough); *Girls and Dolls* by Lisa McGee and *Colourings* by
Andrew Keatley (Old Red Lion); *African Gothic* by Reza de Wet
(White Bear) and *The Wonder! A Woman Keeps a Secret* by
Susanna Centlivre (White Bear/Time Out Critics' Choice Season
at BAC). Derek is one third of paper/scissors/stone.

JAMES PERKINS DESIGNER
Theatre credits include: *Ciphers* for Out of Joint (Bush);
Shiver, Lost in Yonkers (Watford Palace); *Dances of Death*
(Gate); *The Girl in the Yellow Dress* (Salisbury Playhouse);
1001 Nights, Liar Liar (Unicorn); *The Fantasist's Waltz* (York

Theatre Royal); *Lizzie Finn, Floyd Collins* (Southwark Playhouse); *The Hotel Plays*, a site-specific piece at The Holborn Grand; *Matters of Life and Death* (UK tour); *Life of Stuff, Desolate Heaven, Many Moons* (Theatre503); *Stockwell* (Tricycle); *The Marriage of Figaro* (Wilton's Music Hall); *St John's Night, Saraband* (Jermyn Street); *Carthage, Foxfinder, Bofors Gun, Trying* (Finborough); *Orpheus, Troy Boy* (UK tour); *Iolanthe, The Way Through the Woods* (Pleasance London); *Pirates and Pinafore* (Buxton Opera House); *The Faerie Queen* (Lilian Baylis) and *The Wonder* (BAC). James created *Story Whores*. He is a member of Forward Theatre Project and one third of paper/scissors/ stone.

SALLY FERGUSON LIGHTING DESIGNER

Theatre credits include: *Many Moons* (Theatre503); *Slowly* (Riverside Studios); *The Devils Festival* (The Print Room); *Eschara* (Exeter Northcott); *Breakfast with Emma* (UK tour); *Karnival* (The Place); *The Girl with the Iron Claws* (Soho); *Floyd Collins* (Southwark Playhouse); *Red* (BAC scratch season); *Eschara and Shoot/Get/Treasure/Repeat* (Exeter Northcott). Sally is a graduate of Wimbledon School of Art and one third of paper/scissors/stone.

JO WALKER SOUND DESIGNER

Theatre credits include: *Much Ado About Nothing* for ACS Random (Park Theatre); *The Engineer's Thumb* for Dotted Line (Little Angel Theatre Puppetry Theatre). Jo is a creative associate of curious directive where his credits include: *The Kindness of Strangers* (Norfolk and Norwich Festival); *After the Rainfall* (UK tour); *In the Image of You* (West Yorkshire Playhouse) and *Your Last Breath* (UK tour).

GEORGE HIMS STAGE MANAGER

George trained at RADA. Theatre credits include: The 24 Hour Plays – Celebrity Gala (Old Vic); *My Fair Lady, Anything Goes* (Kilworth House); *A Class Act* (Landor); *Twelfth Night, Richard III* (Apollo); *Someone Who'll Watch Over Me* (Southwark Playhouse). Other work includes: WhatsOnStage Awards 2012 and 2013, London 2012 Olympic and Paralympic Opening and Closing Ceremonies.

WILLIAM NEWMAN FOR IOGIG PRODUCTION MANAGER

The IOGIG team incorporating William Newman, Ian Taylor and Olivia Dermot Walsh have built impressive careers in theatre, musical performance and event management including: Glyndebourne, the Royal Opera House, Northern Ballet Theatre, Qdos Entertainment and numerous West End shows. In the past IOGIG have worked on productions including *The Fizz* for W11 Opera; *Land of Our Fathers* for Theatre503; *The China* to Hackney Festival; Grimeborn at the Arcola Theatre; *Othello* for Guildford Shakespeare Company and *Nanny McPhee* for London Children's Ballet at Sadler's Wells. For more information about our services and productions please visit www.iogig.com

PETER HUNTLEY FOR 1505 CASTING

1505 offers a new style of general management for theatre and live performance. 1505 can provide productions with a bespoke package of support that includes casting and recruitment, budgeting, contracts and negotiation, venue and tour booking and accounting and payroll. Recent productions supported include *The Act* (Trafalgar Studios); *In the Next Room, or the Vibrator Play* (St James); *Lizzie Siddal* (Arcola) and *The Island* (Young Vic). www.weare1505.co.uk

PRODUCERS

TURNER & CO PRODUCTIONS
Turner & Co Productions is the company established by
independent producer Claire Turner. Claire has worked for
companies including Fuel, Clod Ensemble, Theatre503,
mimbre, Seabright Productions, Headlong and the Young Vic.
Claire was a Stage One Apprentice from 2012–2013. This is
her second production as an independent producer following
The Island by Athol Fugard, John Kani and Winston Ntshona,
directed by Alex Brown – winner of the JMK Award 2013
(Young Vic).

PAPER/SCISSORS/STONE
paper/scissors/stone are a theatre collective, comprised of
director Derek Bond, lighting designer Sally Ferguson and
designer James Perkins. They work together to create
narrative-based theatre with high visual impact. Productions
include *Shiver*, *Lost in Yonkers* (Watford Palace); *Colourings*,
Girls and Dolls (Old Red Lion); *Trying* (Finborough) and
Saraband (Jermyn Street).

UPSTART
Upstart exists to create compelling and entertaining theatre
which confronts the biggest questions facing the society we
live in. We produce a combination of new writing and devised
work inspired by contemporary issues. As well as working with
playwrights including Dawn King (winner of the NT
Foundation Award for *Foxfinder*), Steven Lally (*Oh Well Never
Mind Bye*) and Jack Thorne (*Let the Right One In*) we
collaborate with theatremakers such as Oscar Mike (*The
Falling Sickness*, *The Situation Room*). Our productions
include *The Situation Room* by Oscar Mike (UK tour and full
run at Shoreditch Town Hall); *The Maddening Rain* (UK tour
and 59E59 Theaters New York, in collaboration with
Darbourne Luff); *Oh Well Never Mind Bye* by Steven Lally
(Union Theatre, London); *Water Sculptures* by Dawn King
(Theatre503 and English Theatre of Bruges).

London's most vibrant venue for new theatre, comedy and cabaret.

Soho Theatre is a major creator of new theatre, comedy and cabaret.

Across our three different spaces we curate the finest live performance we can discover, develop and nurture. The company works with theatremakers and companies in a variety of ways, from full producing of new plays, to co-producing new work, working with associate artists and presenting the best new emerging theatre companies that we can find.

We have numerous writers and theatremakers on attachment and under commission, six young writers and comedy groups and we read and see hundreds of shows a year – all in an effort to bring our audience work that amazes, moves and inspires.

'Soho Theatre was buzzing, and there were queues all over the building as audiences waited to go into one or other of the venue's spaces. [The audience] is so young, exuberant and clearly anticipating a good time.' *Guardian*

We attract over 170,000 audience members a year. We produced, co-produced or staged over forty new plays in the last twelve months.

Our social enterprise business model means that we maximise value from Arts Council and philanthropic funding; we actually contribute more to government in tax and NI than we receive in public funding.

sohotheatre.com

Keep up to date:

sohotheatre.com/mailing-list
facebook.com/sohotheatre
twitter.com/sohotheatre
youtube.com/sohotheatre

Registered Charity No: 267234

Soho Theatre, 21 Dean Street, London W1D 3NE
sohotheatre.com
Admin 020 7287 5060 I Box Office 020 7478 0100

MICROCOSM

Matt Hartley

*For my mum and dad,
who have never stopped looking out for me*

Acknowledgements

I owe a lot of people a lot of thanks.

The brilliant actors who have over the years given up their time to help me hear this out loud: Tom Brooke, Simon Harrison, David Hartley, Brendan Patricks, Felix Scott and Michelle Terry.

Chris, Jenny, John and Phil for bringing it to life so vividly.

Nick Bagnall, Réjane Collard and Will Mortimer who helped me make some sense of it. Claire Turner, Peter Huntley, James Perkins and Sally Ferguson for giving this project more time than they could ever possibly be paid for.

All those who stepped foot in 121. Hinkley Road Guest House. The Peggy Ramsay Foundation. Nick Quinn.

Helen Perry, for all the miles.

And finally Derek Bond for rescuing it from my drawer, championing it to such extremes and assembling such a talented team. Get some sleep now mate.

M.H.

Characters

ALEX, *late twenties/early thirties*
PHILIP, *late thirties/early forties*
CLARE, *late twenties/early thirties*
POLICE OFFICER, *male, late twenties/early thirties*

A forward slash (/) at the end of a line indicates continued speech.

Author's Note

The play is set in Alex's recently modernised kitchen/living room. It is on the first floor of a two-storey building, which has been split into two flats. The ground floor makes up one flat and the first floor makes up Alex's. A large bay window is prominent. Throughout the play we should be able to hear the sounds from outside the flat: traffic, passers-by, etc. Key sounds are indicated.

A heatwave is in full force.

This text went to press before the end of rehearsals and so may differ slightly from the play as performed.

Day 1

ALEX *is at the door.* PHILIP *stands in the doorway. In one hand* PHILIP *has a bottle of wine (wrapped with a ribbon) and in the other hand a wing mirror.*

PHILIP. This has really thrown me.

ALEX. Is that mine?

PHILIP. It was a welcoming gift: the wine. To say hi and welcome.

ALEX. Thank you.

PHILIP. Welcome to the area, hope you're settling in okay. But this you know, you just don't cater for this, do you?

ALEX. No. That's my wing mirror isn't it?

PHILIP. The little blue car outside.

ALEX. Yes.

PHILIP. Well yes, if that's your –

ALEX. It is.

PHILIP. Sorry. I'm Philip by the way. I live next door.

ALEX. Erm could I have it please?

PHILIP. Of course. Course, yes. Sorry, holding on to it like it's a newborn –

ALEX. Philip.

PHILIP. Yes.

ALEX. Next door.

PHILIP. Number twenty-two. It's not a flat.

ALEX. Right. Alex.

PHILIP. Alex. Nice to meet you.

ALEX. This is awkward isn't it?

PHILIP. Not the best introduction, is it really?

ALEX. No. But thanks for being / honest.

PHILIP. Just being neighbourly. Honest?

ALEX. Yeah. Shall I just drop the bill round?

PHILIP. Sorry?

ALEX. For the repairs. Once the garage have fixed it.

PHILIP. No, no, no, no.

ALEX. What, cash?

PHILIP. I think there's been a misunderstanding.

ALEX. This is from my car?

PHILIP. Yes, but I think we're, do you think I hit your car?

ALEX. That's what you're saying.

PHILIP. No, no, I was just coming round to say hi, welcome as I was saying before and this was on the floor by your car. So I thought it was best to bring it up.

ALEX. So you didn't hit my car?

PHILIP. No, god no, that would have been awkward wouldn't it? First impressions. (*Beat.*) That's what you thought, isn't it?

ALEX. You did have it in your hand.

PHILIP. Yes.

ALEX. And a bottle of wine in the other.

PHILIP. A welcome gift.

ALEX. Not an apology?

PHILIP. No. No, obviously I'm sorry but it was just I was coming round anyway, so I thought it's best to bring it up.

ALEX. I assumed /

PHILIP. I know.

ALEX. / that you had done it.

PHILIP. I should have clarified.

ALEX. No, I should have…

> *Pause.*

> You definitely didn't do it?

PHILIP. No.

ALEX. No?

PHILIP. No.

ALEX. Sorry. Sorry. I just…

PHILIP. It's okay.

ALEX. Can you see why I…?

PHILIP. Of course, course, yes.

ALEX. Sorry. (*Beat.*) So someone else has done this?

PHILIP. Yeah.

ALEX. Just driven into it /

PHILIP. Well –

ALEX. / and not left their details.

PHILIP. No, no, no, no.

ALEX. They've left details? At least –

PHILIP. No. No. No details. Nobody's driven into it.

ALEX. What?

PHILIP. Not unless they went along the pavement, drove along the pavement. No. Sorry. Sorry, let me explain, it's been ripped off. Vandalised.

ALEX. Vandalised?

PHILIP. I know. Terrible isn't it. Just ripped off. Or out, whichever way you say it. Off I think. It's been ripped off hasn't it?

ALEX. Fucking hell. Sorry.

PHILIP. Don't worry I know how… fucking… frustrating it can be.

ALEX *has gone to the window and is looking out.*

ALEX. Is there any other damage?

PHILIP. You mean like…

ALEX. Scratched. Has it been scratched or broken in to?

PHILIP. No, no not from what I could tell.

ALEX. Has this happened before?

PHILIP. Not that I'm aware of. Certainly I've never –

ALEX. And mine was the only –

PHILIP. Sorry, sorry to interrupt. Can I come in?

ALEX. What?

PHILIP. I didn't want to just walk in. I wasn't sure how long this conversation was going to go on so I've stayed in the doorway, so I'm not sure if I should come in or not but if we are…

ALEX. Of course, of course come in. Sorry I should have –

PHILIP. I just didn't want to carry on talking right across the room but if we are…

ALEX. No, I under–

PHILIP. And I would have started to think about that more, the longer I stood here.

ALEX. Please, just come in, please.

PHILIP. Thank you. Should I take off my shoes?

ALEX. No, no, you're fine. It was, it is Philip?

PHILIP. Yes, Philip Freeman and it's Alex?

ALEX. Yes, Alex Reeve.

PHILIP. We should shake hands.

ALEX. Yes, yes, of course, yes.

They shake hands.

Alex.

PHILIP. Philip. I'm really sorry that this is how we had to meet. I hope you don't assume I'm going to be a bad omen.

ALEX. No, god, no. It's just one of those –

PHILIP. Unlucky things.

ALEX. Exactly.

PHILIP. Frustrating.

ALEX. Yes.

PHILIP. But unlucky.

ALEX. Yes.

PHILIP. Well welcome to the street.

ALEX. Thank you.

PHILIP. If you need anything. Any help with the, just –

ALEX. Thank you.

   CLARE *enters, she has a carrier bag with a few groceries in*. PHILIP *is still holding* ALEX*'s hand*.

CLARE. Oh hello. Hi.

PHILIP. Do you know this person?

ALEX. Yes, yes I do know this person.

   ALEX *manages to prise his hand from* PHILIP*'s*.

   Philip, this is Clare. Clare, Philip. Clare, Philip lives next door.

CLARE. Hi, lovely to meet you.

   CLARE *goes to shake hands with* PHILIP *but* PHILIP *is off on another train of thought and doesn't shake her hand*.

PHILIP. Oh are you… /

ALEX. Yes.

PHILIP. / family?

CLARE. No, Alex, we're not family.

ALEX. No sorry, Philip, we're not family. I thought you were going to say a couple, or living together, that's what I assumed. Not…

PHILIP. You're quick at assuming aren't you!

ALEX. Today I am.

CLARE. Have I missed something?

PHILIP. Just a little private joke.

CLARE. Wow private jokes already, sounds like you two have been bonding.

PHILIP. I think we have yes.

ALEX. Shall we start again? Philip, Clare is my girlfriend and in a week she's going to be living here as well.

PHILIP. Oh right. Lovely. Congratulations.

CLARE. Thank you.

PHILIP. Did you want a bit of time by yourself before she moved in?

ALEX. No. God no.

CLARE. Alex, you didn't sound too sure then.

PHILIP. I picked up a little of that too.

ALEX. I'm very sure. Clare's on nights this week.

CLARE. My flat's right next door to work.

PHILIP. Where do you work?

CLARE. In the A and E at the Royal Free.

PHILIP. Oh are you a nurse?

CLARE. No I'm a doctor. Just. Newly qualified.

PHILIP. Oh. Congratulations. God that's scary.

CLARE. It can be.

PHILIP. You look barely old enough to apply a plaster.

CLARE. Right, I'll take that as a compliment. (*Beat.*) Hot out there.

PHILIP. So I see.

CLARE. Oh god have I got patches.

PHILIP. No need to be embarrassed, apparently it's very healthy to sweat profusely. Cleanses the pores.

CLARE.... Yeah.

ALEX. They're barely noticeable.

PHILIP. Ah look, how sweet, he's still blinded by love. (*Beat.*) What should I do with this?

CLARE. Here let me.

PHILIP. Through here?

CLARE. Or through there...

> PHILIP *is examining the flat.* CLARE *and* ALEX *exchange looks regarding* PHILIP. CLARE *notices the wing mirror.*

> Is this your wing mirror? What happened?

ALEX. Vandalised.

PHILIP. Little hooligans. I found it.

ALEX. I was asking Philip if any others had been damaged when you arrived.

PHILIP. Aren't you two lucky?

ALEX. Erm...

PHILIP. I mean just look at this place. Wow!

ALEX.... oh thank you.

PHILIP. What a lovely, bright, welcoming room. I like the way everything is inclusive.

CLARE. Yes.

PHILIP. Is that what attracted you to here?

ALEX. Well, I suppose that was one of the things.

PHILIP. The area?

ALEX. Yeah, the area and the, the transport links, buses everywhere. Stop so close.

PHILIP. Oh don't start me on the bus stop.

ALEX. No?

PHILIP. No.

CLARE. Okay. Philip, the wing –

PHILIP. Well you know I do try to use buses, journey here and there, my bit towards the environment.

CLARE. That's very conscientious of you.

PHILIP. I know. And we all want easy access to them, but we don't pay what… three hundred and fifty grand…?

ALEX.…Oh. No, no it wasn't that much.

PHILIP. Really? Three-four-five? Three forty?

ALEX. No.

PHILIP. Lower?

ALEX. Well okay if you are going to persist then erm yes it was.

PHILIP. Wowzers.

ALEX. Well we got lucky.

PHILIP. Who did you have to kill?

ALEX. My gran. No well not literally but inheritance.

PHILIP. Well if you paid less than three-three-five for this then…

CLARE. You were saying about the bus stop, Philip?

PHILIP. Yes, yes the bus stop, yes I was, wasn't I.

CLARE. Yes.

PHILIP. She's eager. Well I was saying we don't pay however much to have a bus stop outside our house. You know you want a little bit of distance. It's almost like the yute use them as a scratching post.

ALEX. Do they?

PHILIP. Oh yes.

ALEX. I hadn't actually thought about that.

PHILIP. Don't worry we don't really get any trouble.

ALEX. And I suppose it's not right outside the door.

PHILIP. No. No. No I suppose it isn't it. My wife and I –

CLARE. You're married?

PHILIP. I know, some lucky girl eventually managed to tie me down. Well Sarah and I, that's the wife, we actually had a look round here. We thought, well we were looking into the possibility of getting a second property, little investment, so we had a little mooch around.

ALEX. Right.

PHILIP. We were really impressed.

ALEX. Thanks. My –

PHILIP. But we decided to invest elsewhere.

ALEX. Right. The –

PHILIP. So if you're ever interested in taking a trip to the Dalmatian Coast let me know. All mod-cons. Paint's still wet.

ALEX. Very kind.

CLARE. Yes, very. Almost too kind.

ALEX. Going back to the car though –

PHILIP. Of course yeah, yeah, sorry. Yours was the only one that I noticed any damage having been done to. I suppose that's not really much of a comfort is it?

ALEX. No not really. But it is unusual?

PHILIP. I've never had any trouble but then again I drive a Volvo, they probably thought it wasn't worth the effort.

ALEX. It's just, I don't really understand the want.

PHILIP. No.

ALEX. What you would, would get from this.

PHILIP. I think that's a healthy state of mind. You know not being able to relate to the mindset of the everyday yob. Did you ever watch *Cracker*? Terrible show. I never understood the appeal of it. Or any shows like that, you know where they get inside the mind of the 'killer'? Because who in their right mind would want to be able to relate to a murderer or a rapist? To my mind if you can think like one of them, then you're only one step away from joining them.

ALEX. Well it's just a wing mirror.

CLARE. Alex's right, it's just a wing mirror.

PHILIP. Yes, well, yes. But you know everything starts from somewhere.

CLARE. Still that's a pretty big leap.

ALEX. I think it's probably just boredom isn't it. They don't know any better... circumstances beyond their control.

PHILIP. You're not a hoody-hugger are you?

ALEX. No. No. I'm just, you know in the end it's just a wing mirror, it can be replaced.

PHILIP. That's very reasonable of you.

ALEX. It could be a lot worse, you know at least they didn't do anything more.

PHILIP. Sadly that's the world we live in now.

ALEX. What do you do in these situations? Do I call the police? I know they can't, won't be able to trace anything. But do you report it?

CLARE. I think we just forget about it, Alex.

PHILIP. Last year a fight broke out by the bus stop. Small scuffle. Soon got broken up. Just a couple of black youths. It was all argy-bargy really. A lot of talk, front, I think is what you'd say. But serious threats. Talk of knives and the sort. And I phoned up the police and told them what was going on and do you know what they said? They said: are they still fighting? I said no but it looks like they might again and they said well if they do start fighting again then call. I thought you know, come on, there are times when you have to pre-empt certain things. You know, you don't just watch cracks form on your ceiling and repair it once it's caved in. No, by then it's too late you're stuck under a pile of rubble, if you're not dead that is. You know I'm not saying that I am the biggest fan of the film *Minority Report*, I'm not saying that's what sort of world we should all live in – you look confused.

ALEX. I've not seen that film.

PHILIP. Oh, oh well I'll have to lend it to you. I've got all of his films.

ALEX. Spielberg...?

PHILIP. Tom Cruise.

ALEX. Right, well, thanks.

CLARE. Well you'll look forward to that, won't you?

ALEX. Yes, immensely, thanks, Clare. So, Philip, you don't think I should speak to the police?

PHILIP. I think you just keep these sorts of things to yourself. I think that's what we do these days. Police ourselves in effect.

ALEX. Yeah, yeah.

PHILIP. Yeah.

CLARE. Yeah...

PHILIP. Yeah.

ALEX....yeah...

Silence.

Philip...

PHILIP. Say no more, I understand.

ALEX. Thank you.

PHILIP. Whetted your whistle didn't I? I'll go and get them.

ALEX. Pardon?

PHILIP. The DVDs. Great way to take your mind off this palaver. Don't worry I'll leave the door on the latch.

PHILIP *exits.* CLARE *and* ALEX *stare at each other.*

ALEX. Did that just...

CLARE. Yes it did.

ALEX *goes to the window and watches* PHILIP *leave. He waves out of the window.*

Is it too late to not move in?

ALEX. He's not that bad is he?

CLARE. He likes you.

ALEX. Yes, yes, yes.

CLARE. No seriously, I could see it in his eyes.

ALEX. Very funny.

CLARE. Do you think he did that to your wing mirror?

ALEX. What?

CLARE. It's a great way to introduce yourself. Pop round, act all noble and concerned.

ALEX. No. Stop it, Clare. No. Of course he didn't. (*Beat.*) Do you think? No. No. He's harmless. (*Beat.*) I'm sure he is. (*Beat.*) Don't look at me like that.

CLARE. You're very trusting.

ALEX. Are you winding me up?

CLARE. No, I'm just saying you can search for years trying to find the perfect place to live, study and love the area, the shops, et cetera, yet all of that can be shattered by one crazy neighbour.

ALEX. He's not crazy. He didn't do that, no way. No.

CLARE. Of course, course not. (*Beat.*) I'm going to be late for my shift.

ALEX. Come back here tonight.

CLARE. I'll see what time I finish.

ALEX. Please. This is our first night in our new home.

Pause.

CLARE. Okay. (*Beat.*) Keep your eye out for the nutter.

ALEX. I will.

CLARE *smiles at* ALEX, *she kisses him goodbye and then exits.* ALEX *goes to the window and watches her go, he smiles.* ALEX *then stares round his flat. Blackout.*

Day 4

Early evening. ALEX *is sitting in the dark, watching TV on his iPad, with the curtains closed. On the table we can see a pile of DVDs and the wing mirror.* CLARE *enters. She goes to turn the light on.*

ALEX. Wait!

CLARE. Alex!

ALEX. Don't turn the light on.

CLARE. What are you doing in the dark? Nearly gave me a heart attack.

ALEX. Don't turn the light on!

CLARE. I heard. What you doing? It's beautiful out there.

ALEX. I know.

CLARE. Then why have you got the window and the curtains closed.

ALEX. You'll laugh at me.

CLARE. I'm not laughing.

ALEX. I mean you will when I tell you: I'm hiding.

CLARE. Hiding? From what? (*Beat.*) From Philip?

ALEX. He was trying to invite himself in. I told him I wasn't feeling great and was going to bed. It was the only thing I could think of saying.

CLARE. I'm surprised that stopped him coming round.

ALEX. Barely did. He offered to bring me some chicken soup.

CLARE. Please tell me that's not true.

ALEX. As far as Philip is concerned I am a vegetarian.

CLARE. So this is how it's going to be is it? We're going to turn the flat into a blacked-out sauna because you've gone and got yourself a stalker.

ALEX. Oh don't start.

CLARE. Go on, please let me I could do with a laugh.

ALEX. What's wrong?

CLARE. You don't want me to begin. Seriously. I might never stop.

ALEX. That bad?

CLARE *nods*. ALEX *goes and opens the window*. CLARE *smiles*. ALEX *gestures for* CLARE *to sit down. She does.* ALEX *gets her a drink from the fridge.*

CLARE. Sometimes I wish I could just turn off when I walked out the door.

ALEX. Okay.

CLARE. Apparently, well I'm told you just learn not to let things you see upset you. But at the minute I'm not in that place.

ALEX. Of course you're not.

CLARE. But I will be. It happens to everyone. I can see it. I know in a few years' time I'm going to be a different person.

ALEX. You don't know that for sure.

CLARE. Al, I hope that it is true, not that it isn't. I wish that I was already four, five years more down the line and that I was at the point where I didn't care about what I have to do.

ALEX. What's happened?

CLARE. I've got a face for delivering bad news apparently. (*Beat.*) Two boys. And I mean boys were brought in earlier one of them hadn't even turned fourteen. Anyway, well they'd both been stabbed, one of them died in theatre. Just bled out. Knife hit his axillary artery. Gone. Simple as that. He's just a little boy on a slab now. The other was a bit luckier, and by a bit I mean the slightest margin, because he's still just about holding on. Knife perforated his liver, it was a mess, toxins, poisons that would have escaped, pain beyond imagining, but the bleeding wasn't as profuse. All this, this was all for apparently saying somebody had bad breath. Just some stupid nonsense. Simple as that and it had got out of control. And so the point of this is I was given the task of telling the dead boy's mum. She made this noise… not a sound you'd associate with humans… I just wished that I didn't feel a thing. Because if this is how I feel most of the time I'm doing the job, then it's not something that I think I want to be doing for the rest of my life. (*Pause.*) I don't want you to say anything if that's alright. All I kind of want is a hug.

CLARE *goes to* ALEX *and they hug.*

ALEX. Hello.

CLARE. Hi. (*Pause.*) In years to come this won't hurt me.

ALEX. You don't know that –

CLARE. It can't.

ALEX. Okay.

Pause.

CLARE. Do you promise to love me even if I become a cold-hearted bitch?

ALEX. Of course.

CLARE. Even when I get old and fat.

ALEX. Yes.

CLARE. Because I will, it's in my genes. I'm going to be a fat bitch when I'm old.

ALEX. It's alright I'll have Alzheimer's by then so I won't know who you are.

CLARE. The perfect couple.

ALEX. That's right.

CLARE *smiles.*

Puts my day into perspective.

CLARE. Oh tell me about the PH levels. (*Beat.*) Please.

ALEX. Well I tell you what the lads at work got in a right
    frenzy this afternoon, base-rate PH went down to three point
    eight at Slough's treatment centre. I said to them the shit is
    literally hitting the fan. Not one laughed. They just said yes.
    Yes it has. (*Beat.*) Oh Jesus, listen to me, I'm not saying
    water treatment is glamorous but you'd expect people to at
    least have a bit about them. I need to make some friends
    down here don't I.

CLARE. Well you've got Philip.

ALEX. Oh don't, I keep expecting him to crawl in like one of
    those face-huggers from *Aliens*.

CLARE. Was Tom Cruise in that one?

    ALEX *heads over to the window and peers out.* CLARE
    joins him.

    Don't move. He's there. Looking up. Alex, don't move. He's
    nestled in the hedge.

ALEX. He's not.

CLARE. He is, he's looking right up at you and he's oh wow,
    oh –

ALEX. What?

CLARE. He's having a cheeky tug. Cheeky's actually the
    wrong word. Aggressive, I'd say.

ALEX. Oh stop it. (*Looks out.*) He's not there.

CLARE. Course he's not there. He's odd but he's not hit those
    heights. Yet. You still haven't fixed the mirror.

ALEX. Do you know how much that costs to repair?

CLARE. How much?

ALEX. Well it's not just the mirror it's the electrics, everything
    will need replacing so could be two, three hundred pounds.

CLARE. That much?

ALEX. More hassle than it's worth.

Noise from outside. ALEX *goes and looks out of the window.*

Just some kids. Do you think if I was stood here like this he would have still done it?

CLARE. Philip?

ALEX. It wasn't Philip.

CLARE. Why did you say he?

ALEX. It's more likely to be a he isn't it.

CLARE. I don't know. Some of the things I've seen girls do, I would say it's just as likely.

ALEX. Seriously though, whoever it was do you think they would?

CLARE. I think you'd be surprised how little that would matter to people.

ALEX. I think I'd be a good deterrent.

CLARE. Stop saying stupid things. Seriously. Did you not listen to a word I said about what happened at work today?

ALEX. I did.

CLARE. Good. Now I'm going to have a shower. When I come back can you have put the wing mirror down and have made me some cheese on toast.

ALEX *nods.* CLARE *exits.* ALEX *looks out of the window. The wing mirror still weighing heavily in his hand.*

Day 7

There are a couple of boxes on the floor. CLARE *enters carrying one, followed by* PHILIP, *who is also carrying a box.* PHILIP *is wearing short-shorts.*

CLARE. Just there will be great.

PHILIP. Here?

> PHILIP *puts a box down in a different place to where* CLARE *pointed.*

CLARE. Or there, will be fine.

Awkward silence.

PHILIP. Excited?

CLARE. Nervous.

PHILIP. Don't you think it will last?

CLARE. No, I've never done this before.

PHILIP. Oh. Well you couldn't have picked a nicer man.

CLARE. I think so.

PHILIP. You know, obviously I don't know him as well as you do.

CLARE. Obviously.

PHILIP. But from what I do know of him he seems genuinely decent and –

CLARE. Yes.

PHILIP. And I'm sure that it's going to work out beautifully for you both.

CLARE. Thank you.

Silence.

Nice shorts by the way.

PHILIP. Oh these I just threw them on.

CLARE. Do you go on many safaris?

PHILIP. I do no such thing. I just like the way they feel.

CLARE. Well it'd be a crime not to enjoy the sun whilst it's out.

PHILIP. Yes, yes it's very hot. Can we not be British and talk about the weather it's frighteningly dull. I know small talk is an occupational hazard in your line of work but –

CLARE. I'm a doctor, Philip.

PHILIP. Of course you are yes. (*Beat.*) I should give him a hand.

CLARE. He'll be fine.

PHILIP. You don't want to leave that van unguarded. Can't leave anything unlocked, not even for a moment any more.

CLARE. He'll remember to lock it.

PHILIP. Even in broad daylight some little oik would pilfer something.

CLARE. It will be okay. No?

PHILIP. I'd love to say yes. I really would. I'll just check he's okay. Hold that thought, here's the big man.

ALEX *enters carrying a box.*

ALEX. One flight of stairs and I'm sweating.

PHILIP. It's this heat, it's unbearable. So invasive.

ALEX. We need a storm.

PHILIP. Exactly a good storm. Break this heat's back. Clear the air. Either that or you need a pair of these.

ALEX. Oh, wow, they put the word short in shorts, Philip.

PHILIP. They maximise the leg exposure to the air. I can't recommend them highly enough.

CLARE. Is there anything else to bring up?

ALEX. A couple of things.

PHILIP. Did you lock the van?

ALEX. I think so.

PHILIP. Alex, oh my, think is not good enough. I'll guard the van. You follow. Clare, leave this to us, I'm sure you've got things that you can be doing in here.

PHILIP *exits*.

ALEX. I'm actually lost for words.

CLARE. Just go and do your thing with Philip. Just do that.

ALEX *nods and exits*. CLARE *starts to unpack. Noises outside. A loud scooter and then some voices. Scooter stops and returns. She goes to the window.*

Alex.

CLARE *opens the window.*

Alex!

She exits. We hear voices from outside. Eventually we hear the scooter exit. Soon after, all three enter, PHILIP *carrying a box.*

Is the heat making you go doolally?

ALEX. I'm not doolally.

CLARE. You shouldn't get involved.

ALEX. I wasn't getting involved.

CLARE. You were.

ALEX. He was driving too fast.

CLARE. Philip, was he getting involved?

PHILIP. He was driving too fast.

CLARE. Philip!

ALEX. See he was driving too fast. And I just pointed that out.

CLARE. But you didn't have to carry on.

ALEX. He was the one that stopped and came back.

CLARE. And you told him again.

ALEX. Well I wasn't going to applaud him.

CLARE. Exchanging a war of words with a teenager.

ALEX. He was the one that was swearing.

CLARE. He'll know where you, where we live now. Probably get a whole bunch of his mates –

ALEX. Don't be daft.

CLARE. Do you not watch the news? Alex, I know it's not nice but you've got to be careful. Can't confront people like that.

ALEX. How else do they know they've done something wrong?

CLARE. They know.

ALEX. But what if you'd been crossing the road?

CLARE. I'd have moved out the way. You know you're such a bumpkin you're so scarily naive.

ALEX. No I'm not.

CLARE. Yes you are because if you weren't you'd know you don't get involved.

ALEX. That's a sad state of affairs then isn't it.

CLARE. It's not about being sad it's about the way it is.

Pause.

ALEX. Clare, let's not let this spoil your moving in. It's our special day.

ALEX *puts his arm round* CLARE. *They hug.*

I just want this to be perfect.

CLARE. It is.

ALEX. Hi.

CLARE. Hello.

PHILIP *coughs.*

ALEX. Philip, Philip, let me take that off you.

PHILIP. I didn't want to start putting things on top of /

ALEX. Sorry I should have –

PHILIP. / others in case they were delicate.

ALEX. Leaving you standing there with it.

PHILIP. Here.

ALEX. Thank you.

   ALEX *takes the box and puts it aside*.

PHILIP. You did lock your van?

ALEX. Yeah.

PHILIP. Because you can't trust them. Those –

ALEX. Don't worry I locked it.

   Pause.

PHILIP. Dinner.

ALEX. Dinner?

PHILIP. We'll have to have dinner.

ALEX. …yes.

PHILIP. Fantastic. That'll be fantastic.

CLARE. The four of us.

PHILIP. Four?

CLARE. Sarah. Your wife.

PHILIP. Of course yes. Alex and me, Sarah and you. Four.
   Fantastic!

ALEX. Philip, your films do you want them back whilst you're
   here?

PHILIP. Only if you've finished with them. Marvellous isn't he?

ALEX. He's certainly something.

PHILIP. Which one was your favourite?

ALEX. …this one…

PHILIP. Oh political. *Born on the Fourth of July*. Ironic really
   as did you know Tom was actually born on the third of July.

CLARE. Maybe I should leave you two men to talk about Tom Cruise. It's much more of a man's conversation –

PHILIP. I'm not intruding am I?

CLARE. No, no, no. Please. I can start rearranging the bedroom and I know Alex has got some interesting thoughts he'd like to share with you on some of those films.

PHILIP. Really?

CLARE. Haven't you, Alex?

ALEX. Yes. Thank you, Clare. Very interesting.

PHILIP. Oh fantastic.

> ALEX *mouths at* CLARE: *'What are you doing?' She*
> *mouths back: 'You deal with him, you made this problem.'*

CLARE. Philip, thank you ever so much for your help.

PHILIP. Pleasure. It was nothing. If you ever need anything.

CLARE. Number twenty-two. It's not a flat.

PHILIP. That's right.

CLARE. Thank you.

> CLARE *smiles at* ALEX *and then exits.*

PHILIP. I'm jealous.

ALEX. Sorry?

PHILIP. I'm jealous, Alex. I know it sounds silly but I'm jealous. You. This. Everything's so new. Fresh. I remember that excitement. Butterflies. And tingles. I used to get lots of tingles.

ALEX. Right.

PHILIP. Feels like an eternity ago now...

ALEX. Right.

> *Long pause.*

PHILIP. So you had some thoughts.

ALEX. Philip, sorry. I can't really think about those things just now.

PHILIP. Is your mind still on that argument?

ALEX. He was driving stupidly wasn't he? If anyone had stepped out they would have been...

PHILIP. Dead, yes. Phoebe. Clare. You. Me.

ALEX. Sarah.

PHILIP. Oh yes, yes anyone. It only takes a second. It's unacceptable, there's no place for behaviour like that.

ALEX. But.

PHILIP. Don't try and find excuses for him.

ALEX. I don't think I can in this instance.

PHILIP. Good.

> ALEX *has gone over to the window.*

Any plans for next week? Just that Tom's got a new film out. Thought we could go.

ALEX. Er, yeah. I'll have to check with Clare.

PHILIP. Oh I don't think it's very girly.

ALEX. I'll have to ask though.

PHILIP. She won't be able to say no to that. Two men just watching a bit of Cruise nothing wrong with that. I normally go by myself. It'd be nice to just...

ALEX. Can I let you know?

PHILIP. Of course. Sure. Sure.

ALEX. Do you think he meant what he said?

PHILIP. Of course he knew where you lived you were outside your house. Your front door was wide open. Not really a case for Columbo.

ALEX. The intent I mean.

PHILIP. Look, he was a moron. A little moron. Would you do it again?

ALEX. Tell him to slow down?

PHILIP. Yes.

ALEX. Yes, I would.

PHILIP. Well there you go then.

ALEX. It's just what with that and the group that have been hanging round.

PHILIP. Have you had trouble with them?

ALEX. No. No. No trouble.

PHILIP. But?

ALEX. I don't want to sound...

PHILIP. Oh just say it. They're a plague. Don't be embarrassed about saying that, they're a blight on our street and the sooner they're gone the better.

ALEX. Don't think it's that bad.

PHILIP. Come on, Alex. I moved here because I didn't want that sort of trouble. I spent the money for my family to live in a safe, friendly environment. And I think that you know that you did too.

A moment.

ALEX. People keep telling me I'm a little naive.

PHILIP. Well I suppose you have what people would call the right intentions.

ALEX. What do you mean?

PHILIP. Look I know you want to give everyone the benefit of the doubt, give them an excuse for their behaviour but sometimes a little shit is just a little shit.

ALEX. You just swore.

PHILIP. Look what they do to me. Lose all sense of myself. Alex, it's healthy to think the worst of people. What are you pulling that face for?

ALEX. Just.

PHILIP. Alex?

ALEX. Not everyone's as fortunate as me though.

PHILIP. No but that's not your fault is it. You can't solve the world through feeling guilty at the opportunities you've been provided. Best you can do is embrace it. What is it with people like you feeling guilty? You've done nothing wrong. I blame the parents.

A moment.

ALEX. How old's Phoebe?

PHILIP. Three. She's three.

> PHILIP *shows* ALEX *a picture of Phoebe on his phone. Beat.*

> Have you thought about having a little mini Alex?

ALEX. One massive step at a massive time. But…

PHILIP. But you're not ruling it out?

ALEX. I… God, Philip, you're almost as bad as my mum.

PHILIP. Say no more. Can I tell you something?

ALEX. Sure.

PHILIP. A little thought of mine. I think that you should have to have a licence to have children. Being a bad parent is far more dangerous than being a bad driver. It shouldn't be seen as everyone's god-given right. It's a privilege. So many problems would be stopped if the wrong people were stopped being allowed to breed.

ALEX. That seems a little bit extreme Philip.

> *Sound of a scooter approaching.* ALEX *stares out of the window, watching the approaching vehicle. The sound eventually fades but* ALEX *continues to look out of the window.*

PHILIP. Was that him? Alex?

> *A moment. Blackout.*

Day 16

ALEX *is talking to the* POLICE OFFICER. *Whilst doing this he is making him a drink.*

ALEX. I don't want to sound, sound...

POLICE OFFICER. Paranoid.

ALEX. Well yes but petty as well. You know I don't want to put you out of your way for something that compared to what you're used to dealing with –

POLICE OFFICER. Don't worry.

ALEX. You know you're obviously very busy and it's hardly murder. It's just...

POLICE OFFICER. Why don't you explain to me what's been going on.

ALEX. Okay. Okay. (*Beat.*) Does this go any further, what I tell you?

POLICE OFFICER. Well that's up to you really, sir, and what you tell me.

ALEX. It's just that I don't want my girlfriend to know about this.

POLICE OFFICER. Talking to the police?

ALEX. And some of the things I'm going to tell you.

POLICE OFFICER. Right.

ALEX. I just think it's best not to get her alarmed.

POLICE OFFICER. Does she have cause to be alarmed?

ALEX. Well, this is where I'm not sure if I'm being paranoid or not.

POLICE OFFICER. Okay, well why don't you start at the beginning.

ALEX. Okay. I moved in about two weeks or so ago and since then a few things have happened.

POLICE OFFICER. Like?

ALEX. Well I got the wing mirror ripped off my car.

POLICE OFFICER. From outside.

ALEX. Yeah, it's the blue car, just outside.

POLICE OFFICER. I see. Did you report it?

ALEX. No. No, I didn't. You know I thought what's the point? It's not like you can, well would be able to do anything with it. (*Beat.*) Would you?

POLICE OFFICER. No. But you should still report things.

ALEX. Is there any point if you can't?

POLICE OFFICER. Well for our figures.

ALEX. Okay. Well I just passed that off as drunken idiots. Not a unique or venomous attack on me.

A scooter goes past.

POLICE OFFICER. Mr Reeve?

ALEX. Sorry. So yeah I passed that off as a one-off. But you know obviously it plays on your mind, the fact that it happened outside your own house.

POLICE OFFICER. Of course.

ALEX. And so I was a little bit more wary from then on. And I, well one day I noticed that the car had a scratch down its side. Which I hadn't noticed before. And it looked like somebody had keyed it. That's what you say isn't it?

POLICE OFFICER. If they used a key, yes.

ALEX. Well it looked like that.

POLICE OFFICER. So it's a case of vandalism right? That's what you wanted to report.

People walk past outside. ALEX *takes a moment.*

I appreciate that these things must be frustrating but there's very –

ALEX. Sorry, sorry to interrupt. That's not what the crux of the matter is.

POLICE OFFICER. No?

ALEX. I was just trying to give some sort of context.

POLICE OFFICER. Okay. So this is not what's led you to calling?

ALEX. No. See I don't want to sound really paranoid.

POLICE OFFICER. Please. Just say what's troubling you. Don't worry about how you think you sound.

ALEX. Thank you. So not long ago I was, my girlfriend was moving in, and when I was unloading her things from a van I'd hired, this young man, boy really, drove past on a scooter. I say drove past, more like flying. He was going far too fast for a street this size.

POLICE OFFICER. Okay, too fast. And?

ALEX. Well I shouted at him as he was driving past.

POLICE OFFICER. You shouted?

ALEX. Yeah and made a sort of gesture to slow down.

POLICE OFFICER. And did he?

ALEX. Well yes. He stopped. He came back and started, well we had a disagreement. I told him he was driving too fast. And well he told me to 'go fuck myself' and 'I know where you live' and 'that he would have me'.

POLICE OFFICER. So he threatened you?

ALEX. Well, I didn't really take much notice but yes. That's what he did, he threatened me.

POLICE OFFICER. How long ago was this?

ALEX. Week ago. Bit more.

POLICE OFFICER. And did he physically...?

ALEX. No. No it was all 'talk'.

POLICE OFFICER. Okay. And how old was he?

ALEX. He was wearing a helmet so I couldn't be sure. But I'd say only just old enough to drive if not younger.

POLICE OFFICER. Right.

ALEX. I can't remember if you wanted sugar or not?

POLICE OFFICER. Just one please.

ALEX continues to make the tea.

ALEX. But since then, you know, I don't think his talk of 'I know where you live' was for show.

POLICE OFFICER. Has he been round?

ALEX. Well, I can't say for sure if it's him. Not round but. Right. Sometimes. Somebody's going past on a scooter, beeping their horn, which I assume is him.

POLICE OFFICER. Right.

ALEX. And that's been a little unsettling. Him making his little point. Plays on your mind.

POLICE OFFICER. And it's definitely him?

ALEX. I don't know for sure. You know sometimes I'll just hear that when I'm doing something like I am now. And I won't have seen who it is.

POLICE OFFICER. So you can't be sure that it is the person you had a confrontation with?

ALEX. No. But, you know not many other people beep their horn or drive by quickly.

POLICE OFFICER. It is a fairly busy road though, sir.

ALEX. I know and this is why I mentioned that I don't want to sound like I'm being paranoid. Just that I'm sure he was part of a group.

POLICE OFFICER. Group?

ALEX. Of kids. That hang around on the street and I assume that he was mates with them because they've been loitering around outside, not just outside mine but around and they… they've been shouting things and –

POLICE OFFICER. Like?

ALEX. 'Twat.' Nothing particularly imaginative, just silly words really. But just there's a lot of them doing it.

POLICE OFFICER. I appreciate that this must be intimidating.

ALEX. Well it's much more my girlfriend's safety I'm concerned about.

POLICE OFFICER. Is this what you didn't want to tell your girlfriend?

ALEX. Well she lives here so she's aware.

POLICE OFFICER. So there is something else?

ALEX. Yes. Our wheelie bin has been stolen.

POLICE OFFICER. From outside?

ALEX. Yeah, it wasn't even out on the street. It was taken from our little gated area. So somebody's obviously come through our gate to take it.

POLICE OFFICER. Anything else?

ALEX. My tyres have been slashed.

POLICE OFFICER. Really?

ALEX. Well there was a nail in the front tyre.

POLICE OFFICER. Right –

ALEX. I hadn't moved the car all week.

POLICE OFFICER. Okay well that could be criminal damage.

ALEX. There was something else.

POLICE OFFICER. Okay.

ALEX. Something was put through my letter box.

POLICE OFFICER. What?

ALEX. Shit. Sorry there's no polite way to say it.

POLICE OFFICER. That's disgusting. Through your letter box?

ALEX. Yeah.

POLICE OFFICER. That's just disgusting. I'm sorry that happened to you. (*Beat.*) Was it human?

ALEX. Sorry?

POLICE OFFICER. Was it human or animal? Like dog's mess.

ALEX. Does it make any difference? Somebody put shit through my door. I came home to find shit through my door. My first thought wasn't what orifice or being it came from, it's about what sort of person would do that!

POLICE OFFICER. I appreciate it's disgusting, Mr Reeve. But it would make a difference.

ALEX. Why?

POLICE OFFICER. Well if it was human it would suggest that it was premeditated as you know you don't find much human waste lying round. It would suggest that it was brought especially to do that.

ALEX. I don't know, what it was. Hadn't thought like that. I kind of hope it was a dog going by that information.

POLICE OFFICER. Yes.

ALEX. You know for somebody to carry one of their own turds round with them for the sole intention of dropping it through my front door shows a lot more determination to annoy, offend me.

POLICE OFFICER. Exactly.

ALEX. Yeah.

Silence.

Sorry, your tea, it's probably cold now.

POLICE OFFICER. I'm sure it will be okay.

ALEX. I can do you another one.

POLICE OFFICER. No I'm sure that will be fine.

ALEX. It's no problem.

POLICE OFFICER. This is fine. Thank you.

POLICE OFFICER *takes a sip of his tea.*

That's great. Strangely cooling.

ALEX. I don't know how you cope in all that uniform.

POLICE OFFICER. You get used to it. That and you wear a lot of anti-perspirant.

ALEX. Biscuit?

POLICE OFFICER. No.

ALEX. I've got Jaffa Cakes.

POLICE OFFICER. Okay then. Thanks.

ALEX *offers a biscuit.*

Have you spoken to your neighbours downstairs about this?

ALEX. Downstairs, no. They, well, from what I understand, he, she works abroad at the moment. I've not met them.

POLICE OFFICER. So you feel that you can rule out their involvement.

ALEX. I think, I would say so, yes. (*Beat.*) Do you think I'm being paranoid? It's just that of late, I've been finding myself thinking that every noise, every vehicle that passes, every person that walks by could be about to do something. And I don't want to be like that. I want to be being paranoid.

POLICE OFFICER. If I'm honest you probably are.

ALEX. Good.

POLICE OFFICER. What's going on is despicable. You shouldn't have to worry about your safety in your own home. But you can rest assured, and I'm not claiming this is a good thing because it certainly isn't, but you're certainly not the only resident that I've had this or very similar conversations with. Things, incidents like this are very common.

ALEX. You deal a lot with this?

POLICE OFFICER. I made two similar visits yesterday. And the heat always makes people a little more jumpy. Gets people's temperature literally rising.

ALEX. I don't think I find that reassuring.

POLICE OFFICER. Mr Reeve, from what you have described I don't think you should worry.

ALEX. I don't want to. It's just, you should see them when they're hanging around. A little pack. God I sound like...

POLICE OFFICER. No, you're right. That's what they are.

ALEX. Give it an hour or so once school's out and you'll see.

POLICE OFFICER. I have.

ALEX. On this street?

POLICE OFFICER. You've seen one, you've seen them all really. What I can do is come back later with my partner. Show them we are in the area. Monitoring. Perhaps have a word with them, get them to move on. Because at the moment there's nothing concrete to suggest that it is because of this person or this group. Or both combined.

ALEX. No.

POLICE OFFICER. But we can certainly have a word and monitor what's going on.

ALEX. Thank you, that would be, that would be greatly appreciated.

POLICE OFFICER. Well I better be off. Thank you for the tea and the biscuits.

ALEX. No, thank you.

POLICE OFFICER *goes to exit.*

I hate thinking the worst of people, thinking that it could be them.

POLICE OFFICER. Don't. They don't think about you so don't give them the privilege of your thought. Once again I'm sorry that this is something you're having to experience.

ALEX. It's not your fault.

POLICE OFFICER. It's nice to hear that for a change. Right –

ALEX. Is there anything I can do?

POLICE OFFICER. Sorry?

ALEX. If that doesn't work, if they come back after you've passed by?

POLICE OFFICER. Well try not to think like that.

ALEX. Okay.

POLICE OFFICER. But I suppose what you can do is make a note of anything that you think is relevant or anything you've seen happening.

ALEX. A note, okay.

POLICE OFFICER. And then contact me.

ALEX. You?

POLICE OFFICER. Just contact me via the station. You have the number don't you?

ALEX. Yes.

POLICE OFFICER. Well just call and ask for me.

ALEX. Thank you.

POLICE OFFICER. Right.

ALEX. Should I have a word with them, if they –

POLICE OFFICER. No.

ALEX. No?

POLICE OFFICER. No, leave that to us.

ALEX. Okay. Okay.

    POLICE OFFICER *exits.* ALEX *goes to the window and watches him walk away. Goes to put the mugs in the sink. Blackout.*

Day 20

ALEX, CLARE *and* PHILIP *are gathered around the table, which is laid for four. The window is closed and a fan is in operation.*

PHILIP. I know it sounds ridiculous. But that's what she said.

CLARE. Does she realise we've put a lot of effort into this?

PHILIP. I did say that.

CLARE. Gluten free.

PHILIP. It's what I have to live with.

CLARE. All because I put a bin bag in your rubbish bin?

PHILIP. It does sound silly when you say it like that.

ALEX. This is my fault. I said that you wouldn't mind.

PHILIP. Oh I don't but the way she sees it you might as well have just posted it through the letter box.

CLARE. That is ridiculous. I put rubbish in your bin. I'm sorry.

PHILIP. You could have just put it in your own bin and saved all the trouble.

CLARE. Our bin wasn't there.

PHILIP. Why wasn't your bin there?

ALEX. Oh let's not do this.

CLARE. The council had taken it.

ALEX. Clare –

CLARE. It was broken so they took it back and we were bin-less.

ALEX. Let's just try and forget the bin and everything and just enjoy –

PHILIP. The council took your bin?

ALEX. Yes but let's not dwell on this. Let's –

PHILIP. Well that's very unusual. Normally they just swap them.

ALEX. Can we just stop this? It really isn't that important. The bin wasn't there. It's my mistake.

CLARE. Is she spying on me?

PHILIP. Look I'm not agreeing that her behaviour is normal, anything but, but she did hear a noise right outside our living room, in our garden so it was natural to look out in case anything untoward was happening. What with the yutes that are hanging around. You must do the same?

CLARE. You know she must have made this decision a couple of days ago so why did you let me go to all this trouble?

PHILIP. Well I thought we could still have a nice night.

CLARE. You really should have cancelled, Philip.

PHILIP. I wouldn't have been able to come though. (*Pause.*) Do you want me to go?

ALEX. No, Philip. Stay.

CLARE. Philip, you're welcome please stay. Your company is always interesting. I'm just going to check on dinner.

CLARE *exits*.

PHILIP. Thank you. I don't really want to go back yet if I'm honest. Just nice to have some different company. Even if –

ALEX. Shut up, Philip. (*Pause.*) Sorry. (*Pause.*) Sorry. I shouldn't have said that. That was wrong. Sorry. Sorry. It's just.

PHILIP. What?

Pause.

ALEX. You can't tell Clare. The council didn't take the bin. It was stolen and I found it burnt out round the corner. So I told her a lie because I thought it was best not to alarm her and it's escalated and now it's some sort of big drama which I am sure it didn't need to be.

PHILIP. Burnt out?

ALEX. Yes.

PHILIP. Right. You were just trying not to alarm her?

ALEX. Exactly.

PHILIP. Well there you go. What's the problem?

ALEX. I don't like the deception... even if it's...

PHILIP. Alex, don't worry. I've always found the best relationships are founded on white lies.

ALEX. I'm too stressed to argue with you on that.

PHILIP. Well this fan's not helping. Just regurgitating the same air. Let's open the window up.

ALEX. No.

Beat.

PHILIP. Okay. Why don't you tell me what's getting you stressed.

PHILIP *places his hand on* ALEX's. ALEX *goes to avoid answering the question,* PHILIP *gestures for him to continue.*

ALEX. Well. Just. Well I've started a set of small lies which I thought was for the best. For Clare's benefit but now it's all, well I'm having to dig the lies even deeper. It's only small things but they're escalating.

PHILIP. What like?

ALEX. Well we were meant to go away.

PHILIP. You and Clare?

ALEX. Yes. Go away. Take a trip in the car. But I told her we couldn't because the starter cogwheel needed replacing.

PHILIP. What's a starter cogwheel?

ALEX. Exactly. Nothing. It doesn't exist. I made it up.

PHILIP. Why? Didn't you want to go?

ALEX. Of course I wanted to go. I just didn't want to tell Clare that the reason the car wouldn't move is that the front tyre had been slashed and I hadn't been able to replace it.

PHILIP. You think it was the yob you had an argument with?

ALEX. Yes, well it could be anyone. But I don't want Clare to think that. I don't want to have her worrying about that again. She was really concerned last time.

PHILIP. Maybe you should contact the police.

ALEX. I did.

PHILIP. What did they say?

ALEX. Well there was very little he could do. But he said to keep in contact. And make any notes of anything important.

PHILIP. That's not particularly helpful is it?

Noise from outside.

ALEX. What's that?

PHILIP. It's nothing. Stay put.

ALEX *laughs.*

ALEX. Philip, listen, listen to this, I've even taken to sitting there when I'm in, by the window so I can keep an eye out and occasionally make a note. It's just... it's silly. Really, really silly.

PHILIP. Alex. Don't worry. We're part of one of the finest empires to have existed on this planet. It's our nature to be protective. To watch over our belongings. That's the main reason why we've thrived. Island mentality. So I wouldn't worry about being watchful and protective of something that is rightfully yours to protect. You should be more worried about the little toerags that have been causing all these problems. It's giving me more than a little headache if I'm honest. The way they have been looning about. (*Pause.*) I'm glad you feel that you can talk like this with me.

ALEX. Well I just needed to get things off my chest.

PHILIP. Any time though.

ALEX. How long have you been holding my hand?

PHILIP *withdraws his hand.*

PHILIP. White lies. Don't worry. I think you're doing the right thing.

ALEX. I don't think I am.

PHILIP. Alex.

> CLARE *re-enters. A moment.*

ALEX. Clare. I need to tell you something.

PHILIP. Oh dear.

ALEX. The bins, the car all those things they weren't... they were vandalised and I told you lies because I didn't want to alarm you. I'm sorry, just they were just breeding, all the lies and it's not –

CLARE. Okay. Well you've stopped them now haven't you?

ALEX. Yes.

CLARE. Okay.

ALEX. I want to tell you everything.

CLARE. Good but maybe when we're by ourselves, yeah? Yeah. Philip.

PHILIP. I don't know, you youngsters think that you have to talk about every problem you have. If everyone told all their secrets where would the intrigue in life be.

CLARE. Have you been speaking to Philip about this?

PHILIP. Yes, he has.

> *Noise can be heard coming in from outside.*

> Oh this is a bit awkward isn't it?

CLARE. Yes, Philip, it is.

PHILIP. I'm sorry, Clare, I don't know what it is but people always find me so easy to open up to.

> ALEX *gets up and goes to the window.*

CLARE. This is ridiculous, Alex. (*Beat.*) Alex?

> *Beat.*

PHILIP. Alex?

A loud smash outside.

What was that?

ALEX. Some kids. Chucking bottles about.

CLARE. Don't let them see you.

PHILIP. Let's have a peek.

CLARE. Philip, don't, you'll bring attention to yourself.

> PHILIP *steps back.* ALEX *takes out a notebook from his pocket.*

What on earth is that?

ALEX. I'm just making a note of it.

CLARE. You keep a notebook?

ALEX. Yes.

PHILIP. I'm sure they'll be bored in a minute.

ALEX. Oi! Oi! Oi!

> ALEX *bangs on the window.*

CLARE. Alex, what are you doing?

ALEX. They're right by my car.

> PHILIP *goes back to the window.*

PHILIP. They really are, aren't they.

ALEX. Pass me my phone.

CLARE. Don't call the police it will just make it worse.

ALEX. I'm not. Just going to pretend. Let them see.

CLARE. That's just the same as calling.

PHILIP. Here, use mine.

CLARE. Al, don't go near the window.

> ALEX *stands by the window and pretends to dial.*

PHILIP. What a bunch of brain-dead morons.

> *Sound starts to trail off.*

CLARE. Exactly, they're brain-dead morons who know where we live.

PHILIP. Actually maybe you should sit down, Alex.

ALEX. Well they're going now. Look. Look. Nothing's done.

CLARE. What do you mean 'nothing's done'?

ALEX. Nothing's done. Exactly that. They're gone.

CLARE stares at ALEX.

CLARE. We talked about this.

ALEX. They've gone, I don't –

CLARE. See the consequences. You don't kick a hornets' nest.

ALEX. Clare…

CLARE. Alex, they know where we live.

ALEX. I thought they were going to break into the car.

CLARE. We can't give them a reason to target us.

ALEX. All I want is for you to be safe. I don't want to jeopardise that.

An egg hits the window.

Another.

Shocked looks all round.

PHILIP/ALEX/CLARE. What the – ?!

Another.

A brick comes through the window. We hear noises offstage. Heckling. ALEX checks that CLARE is okay and then PHILIP. ALEX bursts over to the window. ALEX then rushes off.

CLARE. Alex! ALEX! ALEX!!!

Blackout.

Day 20

Broken glass is still on the floor. Blue lights can be seen circling from the road outside. Voices can also be heard. CLARE *and* PHILIP *enter.*

PHILIP. It's not right that. Are we meant to just stand there and say nothing? Do nothing? Just be spare parts? I was just trying to help.

CLARE. Well you weren't.

PHILIP. I was in the room as well.

CLARE. We were all in the room.

PHILIP. I actually saw him throw it.

CLARE. Really.

PHILIP. Well I say him, I assume it was a him, it had a hood over. But the action was manly. Like a cricketer's. A fielder. You don't know what I mean do you?

CLARE. I don't think it's that hard to imagine what somebody throwing a brick looks like, Philip.

PHILIP. Don't lash out at me. I'm a helper here.

Beat.

CLARE. I need a drink.

PHILIP. Me too.

CLARE *pours herself a drink. She leaves the bottle for* PHILIP.

CLARE. Look at all the glass.

PHILIP. I know, it's a miracle no one was hurt. Just missed me by inches.

Blue lights are turned off.

CLARE. I don't know what to do with a broken window.

PHILIP. I'll call somebody for you.

CLARE. Thank you. This is all because of that stupid argument. I told him not to get involved.

PHILIP. I think he's right, he's standing up for what he believes in. He's standing up for both of your rights. Banging on your window when a group of youths are just about to damage his car doesn't make him a bad person. It makes him very, I hope, normal.

CLARE. I just don't want him to get hurt. Did you see the way he ran off? What did he think would happen if he caught them?

PHILIP. There's a difference between chasing people that aren't there and confronting people that are though, isn't there?

CLARE. Obviously but…

PHILIP. You think he would have done something if they were still outside?

CLARE. I don't know. They would have torn him apart. Alex thinks that it's like when we were young. You know, if we mucked about someone would report us to our parents and we'd get in trouble. And we'd live in that fear. So we knew our limits. But he doesn't realise that it isn't like that out there.

PHILIP. That most of them don't care. No empathy.

CLARE. Exactly, no empathy. He's stuck with the mentality of knowing right from wrong but in a time when if you act on it you get punished. What do you do in that situation?

PHILIP. And you know it's only going to get worse. Imagine what it's like when they start to have children, when they have children that age.

CLARE. I know.

PHILIP. What do you think they would say if the police turned up at their door to tell them about their children's poor behaviour.

CLARE. My gut feeling is 'fuck off'.

PHILIP. Well it would be rude yes. We'll have a generation parented by those who have never been properly parented themselves.

CLARE. Parented themselves, exactly.

PHILIP. It can only get worse.

CLARE. I know.

PHILIP. It makes me think, Clare, that what we need is another war. We haven't had a proper war with mass casualties for a long, long time. Iraq is there I know but it's not the Battle of the Somme is it? Not Normandy landing. It's the locals that are dying in the hundreds of thousands not our lot. Clare, it's all about scale. World War Three. If a war of that scale was going on then that's where they would be. Out there. Fighting. That's what they did in the past. Throughout the time of the Empire. Through both world wars. All our young stupid men. Rounded up. Sent out there. Fighting. Dying, yes I know it's tragic but at least Clare it would be for something worthwhile. Freedom. Protecting their country. Not looning about on the streets. Punching and stabbing each other, just for the sake of it. Yes, another world war, it would be population control at its best.

Silence.

CLARE. Philip, that's really scary what you're saying.

PHILIP. I know.

ALEX *enters.*

There he is. All sorted?

ALEX. Is everyone okay?

PHILIP. Bit shaken but I'm a trooper.

ALEX. Clare, you're shaking.

CLARE. I was scared you'd get yourself killed.

ALEX. Sorry.

The POLICE OFFICER *enters.*

POLICE OFFICER. Evening.

ALEX. This is Clare, my partner.

CLARE. We know each other.

POLICE OFFICER. Hospital. Small world.

ALEX. Right. And this is Philip who lives next door.

PHILIP. You didn't need to see where all the glass went?

POLICE OFFICER. No. Is that what they threw?

ALEX *has passed the brick to the* POLICE OFFICER.

PHILIP. I saw him do it. It was like a fielder's throw, in cricket.

POLICE OFFICER. So would you be able to recognise him?

PHILIP. Well the only way I knew it was a boy was because of the way he threw it. Not girly. But I can tell you this it's one of the ones that have been causing trouble.

POLICE OFFICER. I understand that there have been problems.

PHILIP. Yes. I was there when they started. That idiot on the scooter.

POLICE OFFICER. Mr Reeve has brought them to my attention. And I have spoken to them about this issue.

ALEX. And since then it's got worse.

POLICE OFFICER. I'm sorry that you feel like that. But I think it's likely to be a coincidence.

ALEX. Really?

POLICE OFFICER. Yes.

PHILIP. Well is there anything you can do?

CLARE. Philip.

PHILIP. Well I live next door. What happens outside your house happens outside mine as well.

CLARE. Philip, let him speak.

PHILIP. I've got my daughter to worry about.

POLICE OFFICER. We're going to keep a close eye on this issue. But at the moment there's very little we can do.

PHILIP. Can't you speak to their parents?

CLARE. We're not in Surrey.

PHILIP. What about ASBOs?

POLICE OFFICER. We don't issue them any more. They merely moved it onto someone else's door.

PHILIP. And? (*Beat.*) Can you guarantee that my daughter, all of us here, are going to be safe?

POLICE OFFICER. I appreciate that this has been very frustrating.

PHILIP. Can you?

POLICE OFFICER. We can deter such action from happening.

PHILIP. But you can't guarantee?

CLARE. Alex?

ALEX. I can see them. They're at the end of the street. They're just at the end of the street. Watching.

POLICE OFFICER *goes to the window and looks out.*

POLICE OFFICER. Stay inside. I'll go and have a look.

ALEX. Are they just letting me know they're there? Is that what they're doing?

CLARE. Please, can you not, you'll just make it worse. We just want to forget about it.

POLICE OFFICER. It will be fine.

POLICE OFFICER *has exited.*

ALEX. That's what they're doing. They're just standing there.

CLARE. Alex, come away from the window.

ALEX. Watching me, watching them. Are they making a point? Is that what they're doing?

PHILIP *moves away from the window.*

CLARE. I don't know.

ALEX. Why, why are they doing that?

CLARE. I don't know. Alex, sit down.

ALEX. I don't understand.

CLARE. Alex, come and sit down.

ALEX. I just don't get it.

Blackout.

Day 24

The window has been replaced. ALEX *is talking to the* POLICE OFFICER. CLARE *is sat down.*

ALEX. It's the first time I've felt…

POLICE OFFICER. Intimidated.

ALEX. Yeah, I've felt anxious before. But that's different isn't it?

POLICE OFFICER. You were concerned for your physical well-being.

ALEX. I don't expect to have that sort of experience right outside my own door.

POLICE OFFICER. You shouldn't.

ALEX. I was actually scared of a group of people half my age.

CLARE. Tell him why they did it.

POLICE OFFICER. How do you feel now?

ALEX. Better. I feel better /

POLICE OFFICER. Good.

CLARE. Tell him.

ALEX. / I'm inside. I know I'm fine. I know they can't come in here. And you've eventually come round so.

POLICE OFFICER. I did come round as soon as I could.

ALEX. Well it would have been nice if you could have come round quicker. I don't know what's going to happen next time I'm outside.

POLICE OFFICER. Don't start guessing.

ALEX. If they waited for me once.

POLICE OFFICER. They were waiting for you?

ALEX. Well they were outside. Not right outside the gate but I had to go through them in order to get in. Imagine if it had been Clare.

CLARE. Oh don't baby me, Alex.

POLICE OFFICER. You weren't together?

CLARE. I was asleep. I'd just come off a double. The noise woke me up.

POLICE OFFICER. Okay. And they were definitely waiting specifically for you?

ALEX. I'm ninety-five per cent sure.

POLICE OFFICER. Not a hundred?

ALEX. Ninety-five doesn't give you much room for error does it?

POLICE OFFICER. No. How many of them were there?

ALEX. I've got them all on video.

POLICE OFFICER. Sorry?

CLARE. You heard correctly.

ALEX. When I came back in they were still outside so I recorded them so you could see.

POLICE OFFICER. Right. You filmed them?

ALEX. Yeah. With my phone.

POLICE OFFICER. Right.

CLARE. This is the problem.

ALEX. I was making the notes as you said to do but I thought what was the point, when I can actually document it? So now I can show you.

POLICE OFFICER. Have you been doing this a while?

ALEX. A week or so.

CLARE. I told him it was silly, I thought it was too much.

POLICE OFFICER. Let me get this straight you've been video-recording what's going on outside?

ALEX. It's just a natural step on from making the notes, right?

CLARE. Will you tell him that it's not.

POLICE OFFICER. Well if it captures problems then yes it can be used as evidence.

ALEX. Exactly. See.

POLICE OFFICER. But I don't want you to take it too far.

CLARE. Thank you.

ALEX. I'm not taking it too far.

POLICE OFFICER. No?

CLARE. You are, Alex.

ALEX. I feel like there's very little else I can do to be honest. I don't want to just accept these problems. This seems like the most proactive way that I can stop them.

POLICE OFFICER. You can call us. That is what we are here for.

ALEX. Well no offence but by the time you arrive they would have probably disappeared and you won't be able to do anything. These videos are my way of deterring or stopping what's going on.

CLARE. This is the problem though, Alex, you're not deterring it you've been searching for trouble that you wouldn't have noticed otherwise. It's encouraging it by using that phone.

ALEX. No.

CLARE. They play up for it.

ALEX. Look I only filmed when they started doing things.

CLARE. Alex, when does something start? There's a difference between being a nuisance and being a threat and another gap between threat and action and because you're recording them they're threatening you and acting up for your camera.

ALEX. They are the ones in the wrong.

CLARE. It's not about who's in the wrong!

POLICE OFFICER. Alex, can you see that Clare's very concerned about this.

ALEX. I know I know I know that. I…

POLICE OFFICER. Alex? Alex?

Noises from outside. ALEX *listens.*

ALEX. That sounds like it's in the room.

POLICE OFFICER. It's not.

ALEX. I know. But that's how close everything feels.

CLARE. It's okay. There's nobody there.

ALEX. Now I know but…

POLICE OFFICER. Alex, we're here to help you. Yes? Yes?

ALEX. Will you have a look at what I recorded? Please.

POLICE OFFICER. Okay.

CLARE. What are you doing?

POLICE OFFICER. I'm just going to have a look.

ALEX *starts to play a video on his phone.* POLICE OFFICER *reassures* CLARE.

ALEX. Okay. This isn't just from last night. It's always the same group.

POLICE OFFICER. So you've recorded them a few times?

CLARE. Yes, he has.

ALEX. Yeah.

POLICE OFFICER. Did they confront you because of the filming?

ALEX. They said they'd seen me recording them and wanted to know why.

POLICE OFFICER. That's what they said?

ALEX. Not quite as politely, but yes, they had a problem with me recording them.

CLARE. Of course they had a problem.

ALEX. So I told them if they weren't causing problems then I would have no reason to record them. Which is true but they started saying that they weren't causing problems they were just hanging out. But I know that it's not true as I've seen them. I've seen what they're doing with my own eyes and on here. But they were surrounding me, swarming, almost touching me at this point. So I just ran inside. I'm not being over the top am I?

CLARE. Tell him this is over the top.

POLICE OFFICER. Alex, I've been called to situations, where a group of youths, have been sometimes nothing more than a nuisance, and yet they still manage to talk themselves into trouble. It's just a different attitude. Respect is gained by showing no respect.

CLARE. Can you do something with this?

POLICE OFFICER. Obviously I haven't watched it all but there's not much in the way of criminal behaviour in terms of what I'm seeing, if any. Frustrating, yes. But criminal no.

CLARE. There you go.

ALEX. They did intimidate me.

POLICE OFFICER. I know, I know but –

ALEX. You won't do anything.

POLICE OFFICER. Won't is not the right word. Can't. Our hands are pretty tied.

ALEX. I'm sure you've said that before.

POLICE OFFICER. Sadly it's true.

ALEX. Their interests are more important.

POLICE OFFICER. Not at all.

CLARE. Right, well that's that then isn't it. Come on Alex, I've humoured this but look at what it does. This can't happen again. No more filming. Please.

ALEX. Do you agree?

POLICE OFFICER. Well –

CLARE. If he hadn't been recording them then it would have never have happened.

POLICE OFFICER. Maybe. But if it captures something.

CLARE. No, no I'm sorry this is your job to stop crime not his. We didn't sign up for your job. We're not here to monitor, police, even serve the community, we are the community. You can just walk away, we can't. Anything we do, we feel every knock-on. So tell him that it is your job to stop this and for Alex not to record any more.

ALEX. Clare this is my responsibility because if I stop now it will just be giving in and they'll think they can get away with it.

CLARE. You've just been threatened. That was a warning. A wake-up call. So stop. Just please stop now.

Silence.

They threatened you Alex. Am I just talking to myself? Are you going to be able to do anything with this?

POLICE OFFICER. Not as it stands.

CLARE. Okay. So will you leave as I don't want them to see that you've been here.

POLICE OFFICER *exits*. ALEX *and* CLARE *stare at each other*. ALEX *looks out of the window*. CLARE *continues to look at* ALEX. *Blackout*.

Eggs hit the window.

Again.

Again.

A tripod and camera are set up looking out of the window.

Day 29

Night-time. Eggs are splattered across the window. ALEX *is at the window recording. Noises coming from outside. We hear footsteps coming up the stairs,* PHILIP *enters with a few bags of shopping in his hand.*

ALEX. What did they say to you?

PHILIP. Say?

ALEX. I saw them saying things to you.

PHILIP. Can I at least put these down before –

ALEX. Philip.

PHILIP. They asked where I got my sandals.

ALEX. They asked you where you got your sandals?

PHILIP. Well they are nice sandals.

ALEX. Yeah but I can hardly see them wearing them.

PHILIP. No but it doesn't seem to stop them appreciating a good pair of sandals. Where do you want me to put your food?

ALEX. Just there.

PHILIP. Interesting set-up you've got here.

ALEX. So you get asked where you got your sandals and I get asked if I think I'd look good with a knife in my cheek.

PHILIP. God's sake. No wonder you don't want to go outside.

ALEX. I want to go outside. It's that I can't at the moment. Just look at them.

PHILIP. I think you should come away from the window.

ALEX. Am I not allowed to look out of my own window now?

PHILIP. Alex, just come away. You're tense.

ALEX. Of course I'm tense.

PHILIP. I have seen you looking better. I don't mean that in a rude way I meant it out of concern.

ALEX. Being concerned is such a useless emotion, Philip. It's just about the most inactive thing you can do. 'Oh I'm concerned', well do something about it.

PHILIP. I did just go to the shops for you. It's okay. I'm used to being snapped at. I just don't expect it when I come round here.

ALEX. Thank you. Should look in my cupboards, virtually empty. I've been living off crackers.

PHILIP. Don't worry I never believed the saying you are what you eat. Where's Clare?

ALEX. Visiting her parents.

PHILIP. Is everything alright with you two?

ALEX. I just didn't fancy the journey.

PHILIP. You would tell me if it wasn't? I tell you what you need. A neck-rub.

ALEX. No. No, I don't.

PHILIP. Okay. Well I would really advocate getting some air into this room. Clammy and there's a slight pong if I'm being honest.

ALEX. What's your bright idea for that then?

PHILIP. Opening windows are a classic starting point.

ALEX. The window you just told me to stay away from. The window that I have to keep shut because if I open it I get things thrown through it. That window?

PHILIP. You have a point, I take that back.

ALEX. Think I want to be in a sweat-box.

PHILIP. What are you doing now?

ALEX. Backing this up.

ALEX has removed a memory stick and backed it up to his computer. He takes a few items from the shopping bags and starts to make himself a sandwich. He uses a very large knife to do this. Occasionally when he gestures he obliviously uses the knife.

PHILIP. You don't think you're taking this a little too far do you, all this recording?

ALEX. Is that what you think?

PHILIP. It does strike me as a little extreme.

ALEX. I thought this would be right up your alley.

PHILIP. My alley?

ALEX. Monitoring.

PHILIP. Don't get me wrong I think they all should be tagged and gagged until they can act like proper human beings but I mean from a personal point of view. This is a big investment in time and by the looks of it energy for something that isn't having any results.

ALEX. They will help.

PHILIP. Alex, the police can't act on anything that you record as they have no power. The law favours these toerags because the bloody human rights brigade have stitched us up. It's not your fault.

ALEX. What can I do though? I can't not do anything. I'm a man, I'm meant to protect my home.

PHILIP. Well I hate to say it if things get too bad you can always move, it's something I'm considering if things continue like this. Sadly it's the only way I can see myself solving this problem.

ALEX. I can't move.

PHILIP. Why not?

ALEX. Well for a start I'm financially stuck here. We're locked in to a four-year mortgage. We can't go anywhere. And anyway we shouldn't be driven from our own home. I'm not running. This is my home. That can't be the solution. Can it? It can't be? So these clips will have to work. They will work. They will capture something, something that they can act on and the police will stop it and things will go back to normal. Because –

PHILIP. Will you please put that knife down.

Silence.

ALEX. I'm not trying to threaten you.

PHILIP. Just put it down.

ALEX *does.*

ALEX. I wasn't threatening you.

PHILIP. Okay.

Silence.

ALEX. Do you not believe me?

Silence.

Philip?

PHILIP. I think I should leave.

PHILIP *takes a step away from* ALEX.

You need to get some distance, a break from this, as I saw someone different just then, someone who wasn't my friend.

ALEX. Friend?

PHILIP. I thought we were friends.

ALEX. We're neighbours.

PHILIP. All I'm trying to do is help you.

ALEX. Come on you're a grown man who is obsessed with Tom Cruise, why would I want your help.

Silence.

PHILIP. Right. (*Pause.*) I'll show myself out.

PHILIP *exits.* ALEX *stares out of the window. Blackout.*

Another tripod and camera are set up pointing out of the window.

Violent sounds of a group screaming abuse as they kick at ALEX*'s door.*

Day 33

ALEX *is showing the* POLICE OFFICER *a clip of several youths kicking his door.*

POLICE OFFICER. I see.

ALEX. Just there.

POLICE OFFICER. I know.

ALEX. My door.

POLICE OFFICER. Yes.

ALEX. They're kicking it.

POLICE OFFICER. Yes.

ALEX. Well do something.

POLICE OFFICER. You can't see their faces, Alex. I'm sorry but you can't. They know you're doing this. That's why they've completely covered themselves.

ALEX. No, that's not good enough.

POLICE OFFICER. They're playing for the camera.

ALEX. Watch it again.

POLICE OFFICER. Alex, I've seen it twice now.

ALEX. When did you start calling me Alex?

POLICE OFFICER. You said to –

ALEX. I don't think it's appropriate. This isn't a social call. (*Pause.*) Watch it again.

POLICE OFFICER. There's no point.

ALEX. Because you're not going to do anything?

POLICE OFFICER. That's not –

ALEX. Because you haven't done anything so far. Nothing, despite your reassurances. If anything you've made it worse.

ALEX *plays the video again. The* POLICE OFFICER *stops it.*

POLICE OFFICER. I'm sorry that you feel like that.

ALEX. Sorry?

POLICE OFFICER. Yes.

ALEX. Does that actually mean anything? (*Pause*.) I had this
summer job once working for the local council. I used to
write letters. Letters in response to complaints. We were
taught to write like you speak. Empathise. Empathise but
never accept responsibility. Is that what you're doing?

POLICE OFFICER. I wouldn't be doing this job if I didn't care.

ALEX. I don't believe you. You said that if I did this, that it
would make a difference. You said that.

POLICE OFFICER. I said it would help.

ALEX. And has it? I've been threatened. Undoubtedly they
carry knives. Clare is, is –

POLICE OFFICER. What?

ALEX. She's… we had an argument… you've got to help stop
this. That's my door they're kicking.

POLICE OFFICER. Yes.

ALEX. So please don't say that you can't do anything.

POLICE OFFICER. From what you've shown me there's
nothing that can be used to arrest anyone –

ALEX. That can't be true.

POLICE OFFICER. I'm sorry, it is. It's either that or just people
walking past.

ALEX. No.

POLICE OFFICER. We can't watch them all. We don't have the
resources for what is essentially a trivial –

ALEX. Trivial?!

POLICE OFFICER. I shouldn't have used that word.

ALEX. How you see it though isn't it?

POLICE OFFICER. I visit enough people to know it's anything
but. Look I'll make sure that this area is monitored later. We're

being proactive in this area. It is hard. But it will have an effect. You just have to have a bit of faith in what we're doing.

ALEX. I've done that already.

Pause.

POLICE OFFICER. Look maybe you should just have a break from this place. Have a holiday. Get some rest. Clear your head. Talk to Clare, she –

ALEX. Fuck off.

POLICE OFFICER. Sorry?

ALEX. I don't remember calling a doctor, I called a policeman. Telling me what I fucking need, I need this to stop.

POLICE OFFICER. I appreciate –

ALEX. Stop spinning.

POLICE OFFICER. But I do.

ALEX. You appreciate what it's like to become a prisoner in your own home do you? To not be able to look after a person you love, you appreciate that? Because you just said that this was trivial. How can you appreciate it when you use words like that!?

POLICE OFFICER. That wasn't meant in a personal context.

ALEX. This is my fucking home! I had it all sorted. This was the start of my life. Here. But. Look what's…What sort of place are we in if we can't even feel safe in our own home? Because that's what's going on. I'm trapped in my own home. Scared to go outside my own door. What sort of man does that make me? And you can't do anything. Please do something with these files.

POLICE OFFICER. It'd be a lie to take them.

ALEX. Take them.

Silence.

Take them. (*Pause.*) Please. (*Pause.*) Please. I don't want to be like this. I don't want to be like this. They are taking every good bit of me and twisting it. And if this continues I don't think, I don't think I can take much more of it. I'm worried about what I might do.

POLICE OFFICER. Do?

ALEX. I had an urge to go out there. Just go out there and confront it head-on. They're pushing me that far. Fight fire with fire. Because unless you do something how else can I stop it?

POLICE OFFICER. You're not that person. I know what sort of person you are and you're not that.

ALEX. Please. (*Beat.*) You're not going to help me are you?

Blackout.

Day 37

CLARE *and* ALEX. *The flat is in a bit more disarray.*

CLARE. Look at me.

ALEX. You're making it sound like I want to say it.

CLARE. Go on, say it.

ALEX. I don't want to say it. It's the last thing I want to say but it's the only thing I can say because I can't I just can't guarantee your safety here. I think it's for the best.

CLARE. You want me to leave you?

ALEX. No.

CLARE. That's what you're asking.

ALEX. It's the flat.

CLARE. Which we live in together.

ALEX. And only until this stops.

CLARE. What if it never stops?

ALEX. It will.

CLARE. What if it doesn't though? What happens to us?

ALEX. It is going to stop.

CLARE. What does that mean?

ALEX. Clare, you can't be here.

Voices are heard outside.

CLARE. Don't look.

ALEX. Just need to /

CLARE. Don't.

ALEX. / check.

CLARE. No you don't.

ALEX *does.*

ALEX. It's okay. It wasn't anything this time.

Silence.

CLARE. What did you mean Alex? (*Pause.*) What's going on in there? (*Pause.*) We both need to get away from here. Not just me. We can take a break. We can go on holiday. We've both got leave. We could go to Croatia. Down the Dalmatian Coast, see what Philip's villa is like.

ALEX. That's not going to happen.

CLARE. Anywhere then. Anywhere you want. And when we get back it will have settled down.

ALEX. What if it hasn't?

CLARE. Then we move. We say fuck the mortgage, we rent this out, we find somewhere else.

ALEX. We are not being forced out of our home.

CLARE. It's just bricks and mortar, Alex. This flat isn't what's important, it's you and me, flesh, blood, life that's what's important. We only get one chance at it. We can have thousands of flats.

ALEX. This is our home. It's our right to be safe in our own home!

CLARE. Why are you doing this?!

ALEX. Clare, what does it say about me if I can't protect you against a group of kids half my age?

CLARE. You can't protect me Alex. You can't guarantee my safety, nobody can. I can get attacked on any street, or on a bus, the Tube, walking through the park, in the newsagent's, at any time, Christ's sake at work, think about where I work, are you going to guard me in A and E? No, no you're not and that's life. We can't control other people's actions. That makes you no less of a man and I will never think differently of you for it.

ALEX. But in our own home!

CLARE. Oh for God's sake, Alex, this, all of this is your fault.

ALEX. What?

CLARE. If you'd just ignored it and never got in that argument.

ALEX. He was in the wrong.

CLARE. It's not about being in the wrong, it's about knowing when to keep your mouth shut and not to get involved. That's what world we're in.

ALEX. I don't want to live in that world.

CLARE. Well you do.

Silence.

Don't look at me like that. I'm just trying to help.

ALEX. Help?

CLARE. Yes.

ALEX. Liar.

CLARE. What?

ALEX. You're not helping.

CLARE. I am.

ALEX. What I'm doing is helping.

CLARE. That's what all this recording's for is it?

ALEX. Yes.

CLARE. Which one will do that then? The one on your phone?

> CLARE *picks up* ALEX*'s phone and throws it at him.*

Or the ones on here? Or here? Here?

> *She goes to the tripods and goes to throw them.* ALEX *grips* CLARE, *stopping her from throwing. They wrestle for control.*

ALEX. Stop. Stop.

CLARE. They mean nothing. They mean nothing!

ALEX. Clare. Clare! Clare!

CLARE. Fucking nothing!

> ALEX *pushes* CLARE *very hard into the wall. She falls over. Silence.* ALEX *goes to speak. He can't.* CLARE *gets up and exits. Silence. Blackout.*

Day 38

Night-time. Loud, deafening noises. ALEX *stands at the window.* ALEX *walks out of his flat.*

Thunderstorm.

Day 39

Blue lights circling outside. The cameras and tripods have been put away. ALEX *is sat, facing the door. The* POLICE OFFICER *enters, he is not in uniform.*

POLICE OFFICER. Your door's wide open.

ALEX. They keep coming in and out.

POLICE OFFICER. Right.

ALEX. Your colleagues.

POLICE OFFICER. Yeah.

ALEX. I asked them to shut it. They didn't.

POLICE OFFICER. I can shut it if you like.

ALEX. Yeah.

   The POLICE OFFICER *does so.*

POLICE OFFICER. There we go.

   Silence.

   I understand you asked for me.

   Silence.

ALEX. You look different.

POLICE OFFICER. Just come off duty. Tonight I'm a civilian.

ALEX. Smaller.

POLICE OFFICER. It's the uniform. The vest fills you out.

ALEX. Right.

POLICE OFFICER. Mr Reeve.

ALEX. Alex. Please call me Alex.

POLICE OFFICER. Okay. (*Pause.*) Are you alright?

ALEX. It's so quiet right now.

POLICE OFFICER. No it's not, it's pandemonium out there.

ALEX. It's like the air's been sucked out of the room.

POLICE OFFICER. Mr Reeve?

ALEX. Alex. Call me Alex.

Silence.

POLICE OFFICER. Can you help me?

ALEX. Help you?

POLICE OFFICER. Yes.

ALEX. That's nice.

POLICE OFFICER. I'm aware of the irony. (*Pause.*) Did you see what happened?

ALEX. Can they turn those lights off?

POLICE OFFICER. Alex?

ALEX. I'd like them to turn the lights off.

POLICE OFFICER. That's not going to happen for a while.

ALEX. Oh.

Silence.

POLICE OFFICER. Where are the cameras?

ALEX. I don't need them any more, do I?

POLICE OFFICER. What do you mean?

ALEX. It's over isn't it?

POLICE OFFICER. Over?

ALEX. Yes. They won't come back now will they.

POLICE OFFICER. What's going on Alex?

Silence.

If your cameras caught anything –

ALEX. They did.

POLICE OFFICER. Good. That's good. Well I'll need to take the files.

ALEX. I thought they were of no use? That they were taking it too far.

POLICE OFFICER. I appreciate. I understand that I, the police, are hardly top of your thank-you list right now but this is very, very important.

ALEX. It's always been important. Always. Or is this what it takes for it to be important?

Silence.

POLICE OFFICER. You do know that a young man died out there.

Silence.

Alex?

ALEX. Why should I give you them? What have you done for me?

POLICE OFFICER. This is not about you.

ALEX. Yes, it is.

Silence.

I didn't use the cameras. I used this.

Indicates his mobile phone.

POLICE OFFICER. Thank you.

ALEX *keeps hold of the phone.*

ALEX. I didn't record it from in the flat.

POLICE OFFICER. What do you mean?

ALEX. I went out there, I walked up to him and –

POLICE OFFICER. Stop. I think you should stop talking. Alex, I think you should not say anything to me. Wait here. I need to get a colleague –

ALEX. Don't go.

Silence.

POLICE OFFICER. Alex.

ALEX. Watch it.

POLICE OFFICER. My colleague really should be here –

ALEX. Watch it.

POLICE OFFICER. Okay.

> ALEX *turns on the phone. Presses play. The* POLICE OFFICER *watches.*

ALEX. You see that?

POLICE OFFICER. Yes.

> *The sound of an argument, followed by a scream, can be heard from the phone.*

ALEX. You see it?

POLICE OFFICER. Yes.

> *Sounds of pleading can be heard.*

ALEX. Still watching?

POLICE OFFICER. Yes.

> *Eventually the sound stops.*
>
> *Silence.*
>
> ALEX *presses stop.*
>
> *Silence.*
>
> You just watched it.

ALEX. Yes.

POLICE OFFICER. You watched a boy get stabbed and then bleed to death.

ALEX. Yes.

POLICE OFFICER. You could have stopped it.

ALEX. You mean you could have stopped it.

POLICE OFFICER. No, I don't. This didn't need to happen.

ALEX. Do you feel responsible?

POLICE OFFICER. This is really important.

ALEX. So is my question.

POLICE OFFICER. Give me your phone.

ALEX. Not until you've answered me.

POLICE OFFICER. Just hand it over.

ALEX. Do you have a warrant?

Silence.

POLICE OFFICER. The paramedics told me that he died very slowly. That it didn't have to be that way. The knife went through his liver. It would have been unbearable pain but if they had got to him in time he could have been saved.

Silence.

Did you hear me Mr Reeve? What I just said.

Silence.

ALEX. Do you feel responsible?

POLICE OFFICER. I don't have a warrant. But I can go and get one.

ALEX. And I could delete the file whilst you were gone.

POLICE OFFICER. You wouldn't.

ALEX. I don't want to. Answer my question.

POLICE OFFICER. Do you think I should, is that what you're saying?

ALEX. You were right. I'm not the sort that could confront them. Whatever happened I couldn't. But there are different ways of snapping. Because before I could never have sat there and watched someone die. If you'd stopped it.

POLICE OFFICER. No.

ALEX. If you had made it all go away like you should have done.

POLICE OFFICER. No.

ALEX. If you'd done your job properly.

POLICE OFFICER. No.

ALEX. If it had happened out of the blue, with none of this history, then I wouldn't have just stood there. He would not be dead.

POLICE OFFICER. What do you want me to say?

ALEX. That you got it wrong.

Silence.

POLICE OFFICER. I didn't though Mr Reeve. I went out of my way to help you.

ALEX. Liar.

POLICE OFFICER. You made a decision. You made a clear choice. You made the wrong one.

Silence.

ALEX. You. All of you, everyone, told me not to get involved. You said that.

POLICE OFFICER. You know full well that I didn't mean like that.

Silence.

ALEX. I watched a person die. (*Pause.*) I just watched it.

POLICE OFFICER. Yes you did.

ALEX. I recorded it with the camera. Please accept it. Please. I don't want this to be what I've become.

Silence.

Please.

POLICE OFFICER. I can't.

ALEX. Please.

POLICE OFFICER. I'm sorry.

Pause.

ALEX. No. Of course you can't.

Silence.

What could I have done differently? What should I have done?

POLICE OFFICER. You don't need me to answer that.

Silence.

ALEX. What's going to happen to me?

Silence.

POLICE OFFICER. I will get somebody, somebody who is better qualified to speak to you.

Silence.

I'm going to take the phone.

POLICE OFFICER *takes the phone from* ALEX*'s hand.*

Colleagues of mine will be coming up to ask you more questions. Speak to them.

Exits.

ALEX *stares out.*

The blue lights go out.

Fade.

End.

A Nick Hern Book

Microcosm first published in Great Britain as a paperback original in 2014 by Nick Hern Books Limited, The Glasshouse, 49a Goldhawk Road, London W12 8QP

Microcosm copyright © 2014 Matt Hartley

Matt Hartley has asserted his right to be identified as the author of this work

Cover design: Olegusk/Shutterstock.com

Designed and typeset by Nick Hern Books, London
Printed in the UK by Mimeo Ltd, Huntingdon, Cambridgeshire PE29 6XX

A CIP catalogue record for this book is available from the British Library

ISBN 978 1 84842 398 5

www.nickhernbooks.co.uk

facebook.com/nickhernbooks

twitter.com/nickhernbooks